calm

calm

SECRETS TO SERENITY
FROM THE CULTURES OF THE WORLD

lonely planet

MELBOURNE | LONDON | OAKLAND

the secrets

introduction

Shhh.
Stop.
Listen.

Do you hear it over the ringing of your phone? Turn off the television or pull over the car and listen. Do you sense it? Keep your laptop powered down, or you might miss it.

Now, breathe... Do you feel it? It's right there, both obvious and hidden: calm. Even in our noisy, modern world – more cacophonous than our ancestors could have ever imagined – it's still there.

In Western-influenced societies we have mastered technology but created a virtual hamster wheel of stress in the process. Historians believe we work longer hours and take far fewer holidays than did medieval peasants – and they didn't have to endure hour-long, road-rage-filled commutes.

When exactly did it become a bragging right to not be calm? These days, it is considered a badge of honour in Western culture to be busy, stressed, unavailable. Downtime is so last century. And if you're ever feeling a little bored, don't worry. Just get thee to a smartphone, stat.

However, there's been a resurging call to step away from our whirlwinds of busy-ness. We've developed an almost zombie-like addiction to productivity, and researchers are starting to notice the toll on our health. As are we.

So, is attainment of clarity and peace only possible via a 32-hour flight and a four-day trek to a mountaintop sanctuary in a far-off land devoid of technologies and modern conveniences?

Nope.

At Lonely Planet we're travellers, yet even we are telling you that you don't need to travel to find calm. Of course, you could go to Japan to study the ancient art of bonsai (p15). Or you could buy a single bonsai tree, or even a cactus, at your local nursery. You could study the ancient sport of archery in Bhutan (p103), take an archery lesson back home, or just become one with a pub's dartboard for half an hour. While you might not be able to commune with the horses of nomadic Bedouin tribes any time soon (p13), you can certainly practise a little calming shiatsu on your cat.

If you promise to read the whole book, we'll let you in on the overarching secret right now: serenity is nowhere and everywhere. It's not in a location but, rather, in the search itself. Calm is in the state of awareness some researchers call mindfulness, and that others – athletes, dancers, artists and anyone who gets blissfully lost in an activity – know as flow.

We have begun to track the neuropsychological effect of contemplative states. In fact, several (extremely forgiving) meditating Buddhist monks and Carmelite nuns have consented to being studied inside an MRI machine where researchers watched their brains light up amid positive emotions. We now know that calmer brainwaves can elicit all sorts of desirable changes known as the relaxation response: lower blood pressure, less depression, reduced vigilance and fear, even a stronger brain. And you don't need to join a religious order to benefit.

The collection of traditions in this book is not definitive, but a sampling that showcases the diversity of the world's approaches to calm. It is also a practical ideas manual. We've avoided some obvious practices, such as yoga and t'ai chi, offering instead unexpected activities that you might not immediately associate with calm.

The lessons and secrets herein cater to our different needs as individuals. While one person might find calm in raw nature, gliding through water in an Inuit kayak (p11); another might crave the orderliness of feng shui (p105). Or perhaps relinquishing control in a safe environment speaks to you, such as when dancing backwards during an Argentine tango (p99) or transcending individual consciousness in West African *djembe* drumming (p47)? For some, calm is achieved through repetition and ritual, exemplified in two traditions as different as the Sufi whirling dervish (p59) and British high tea (p107). And yet others find calm in simply writing down their thoughts in a journal (p111).

Just like exercise for its own sake wasn't invented until it needed to be, neither was this concerted search for calm. Before we had electric lights, downtime was ingrained in the laws of nature. While post-sundown rest is a necessity in parts of the Gambia (p65), most of us can stay plugged in 24/7.

But what our modern society has taken away, it can give back. We can read about and incorporate into our lives lessons in calm from around the world. And maybe, one day, we can travel to experience a few. There's nothing like a journey to put your own problems into perspective. And when you're in the airport security line? Just remember to take a moment, and breathe.

nature

Glide into Nature

Secret Become one with your surroundings

Tradition Kayaking **Date** Any time **Originated in** Greenland, USA and Canada

Our Western culture is remarkably removed from nature. It's no exaggeration to suggest that many an urban or suburban dweller can go days, weeks or even months, without interacting with the natural world.

Contrast this with ancient cultures, or cultures that have an intimate connection with Mother Nature. Inuits, living in unforgiving sub-zero climates, have been using the intricately designed *qayaq*, or kayak, for at least four thousand years. These kayaks were a core part of daily life, used to transport and move goods, and for hunting and fishing. In some societies a man would build his kayak based on his exact physical measurements; the kayak considered to be an extension of his body.

Perhaps unbeknown to ancient tribes, kayaking hits the modern stress-relieving jackpot, offering exercise, nature, water, relaxed repetitive movements and mind–body cohesion. In fact, trauma therapists have found that bilateral stimulation – such as the movement of kayaking, rhythmically and steadily rowing left, right, left, right – can shift perspectives and relieve long-held anxieties. Furthermore, immersion in an environment of soothing water and fresh green forests restores our peace of mind.

Today, this Arctic export is offered all over the world; you can rent kayaks or go on guided trips wherever there's water. Kayaking won't become your livelihood, but that feeling of becoming one with your boat and, by extension, the natural world…? Row with that.

Creature Comforts
Secret Make an animal friend

Tradition Bedouin horse-keeping Date Any time
Originated in Arabian Peninsula

Our big, complex brains think up big, complex problems, and when we're feeling overloaded other people can be just as exhausting as our own busy heads. When such a feeling hits, there's nothing to beat the best listener of all: an animal pal. Not only are animals marvellously free of judgement, their company reminds us of how easy life can be when you focus on simple pleasures. After all, there's nothing like a good meal and a belly rub.

In the unforgiving deserts of the Arabian Peninsula, Bedouin tribes developed traditions to survive their stark environment. One of these was animal husbandry, and the bond between Bedouin and horse was particularly strong. The Arabian horse – the ancestor of today's breed – was revered for its speed, endurance, courage and loyalty, and was regarded as a gift from Allah. Equestrianism was considered one of the most important parts of *furūsiyya*, the warrior's arts, and the horse was celebrated in poetry and song.

Not everyone can own an Arabian stallion, but perhaps you could give a dumped cat or dog a new lease on life and a loving home. Even some time spent watching the birds flitting among the trees or a spider spinning its web can lift you out of your mental maze and tune your ears to nature's gentle call.

Life in Miniature

Secret Nurture a living thing

Tradition Bonsai Date Any time Originated in Japan

Bonsai is the ancient and charming Japanese art of training miniature trees into aesthetically pleasing shapes. It requires meticulous pruning of the roots and crown, and the wiring of branches to produce a perfect representation of a fully grown tree.

The design of the tree in its pot is deliberate, with shape, colour and texture working harmoniously to express the artist's vision and personality. Beautiful bonsai pieces are treasured and, with proper care, can last for generations.

Practising bonsai requires concentration, patience and taking a long-term view rather than expecting an instant reward, all of which undoubtedly contribute to a meditative state of calm.

However, bonsai is more than this. It involves developing a relationship with another living thing. The bonsai artist must study the miniature tree to understand where it wants to go, and gently train its natural impulses in the direction he wishes to take them. Watering, feeding, planning and, above all a time commitment, mean that the tree becomes an object of devotion.

It's possible to create a similar sense of connection to another living thing through nurturing a pot plant, a whole garden or a pet. Children, of course, provide the ultimate opportunity to nurture – despite not generally inducing calm! But spending time with any living thing, inter-acting and responding to feedback, will create a fulfilling sense of responsibility for another's wellbeing, and maybe help eliminate the anxiety in your life.

Reap What You Sow

Secret Be self-reliant

Tradition Gardening for self-sufficiency Date Any time
Originated in Chartreuse Monastery, France

It's interesting that in this age of mass-produced, processed and supermarket food, homegrown and locally made is making a comeback.

Carthusian monks have understood the wisdom that can be found in a garden since their order was established more than one thousand years ago.

The Carthusian monastery, or Charterhouse, is traditionally designed as a series of small cells around a central courtyard. Each cell has its own walled garden and the monk inside lives alone, praying, writing and tending his garden. This prayerful engagement with God's creation is also a source of food for the monastic community.

By the eighteenth century, the monks had become famous for their liqueur Chartreuse, produced by distilling a secret combination of their homegrown herbs, which they sold in order to buy anything they couldn't grow themselves.

So pour yourself a nip of Chartreuse, grab your spade and head outside. Food tastes better when you've grown it yourself, and the exercise, fresh air and beauty of the garden create a sense of calm self-sufficiency that money can't buy. Share your bounty with your neighbours or create a common garden and build a sense of community – another cornerstone of spiritual health.

The Power of the Catnap

Secret Make sure to get your rest

Tradition Siesta Date Any time Originated in Spain

Sleep is perhaps the most mysterious and the most vital contributor to our wellbeing. The ability to get proper rest is both indicative of, and essential to, a peaceful mind. As Shakespeare put it, sleep 'knits up the ravelled sleeve of care'.

So powerful are its healing and regenerating properties that even taking a moment to close your eyes and allow your brain to fall still seems to mimic its effects, refreshing you in seconds.

In Mediterranean countries, taking time out during the day is enshrined in the tradition of siesta.

Although the observation of the siesta is slowly eroding under modern business pressures, the rhythm of daily life was once built around it, and in countries such as Spain it is still prevalent, especially outside the big cities.

The siesta may have begun as a way to avoid the height of the afternoon sun, but it is also a different way of conducting life – one that involves an early start, a return home for the main meal of the day and some family time, then a doze or rest.

It's not hard to take ten or fifteen minutes out of your busy day for relaxation, be it a brief meditation, a quick nap or even closing your eyes at your desk.

Our bodies are kind to us; even a fleeting salute to the idea of rest is rewarded with a more relaxed mind

Climb the Mountain

Secret Conquer your goals

Tradition Mountaineering Date Any time Originated in Tibet and Nepal

There is an undeniable element of spirituality to the sport of mountain-climbing. Perhaps it's the clear air and the heaven-and-earth views, or the tangible sense of being close to the limit, both physically and mentally. Himalayan climbers such as Reinhold Messner speak of summitting – the act of reaching the top – with almost religious devotion. The message is clear: conquering a mountain takes almost everything out of you, but gives something immeasurable and wonderful in exchange.

So what is that immeasurable quality? Does pitting yourself against a pitiless mass of rock and ice really deliver profound spiritual truth? The idea of 'climbing the mountain to find the truth' is so entrenched it has become a movie cliché, from *Batman Begins* to *The Golden Child*. The reality is probably more prosaic. What you will discover en route to the top are your personal limits – what you are capable of and how deep you are willing to dig to achieve your goals.

'Climbing the mountain' can serve as a metaphor as well as an actual activity. Setting out to do something you have never tackled before can deliver the same kinds of insights as hauling yourself up Mount Everest. It could be running a marathon, starting a new career or standing in front of an audience for the first time.

Summit conquered or fear conquered, you'll learn a little bit more about what you are made of.

The Trick is to Stop Breathing

Secret Control your breath

Tradition Free-diving Date Any time
Originated in Sulawesi, Indonesia and the Sulu Sea, Philippines

When we're stressed our body clicks into hyper mode: the heart races, the pupils dilate and breaths come fast and shallow. It's a vicious circle – the quicker you gasp for air, the more panicked you get. That's why we're taught that breathing exercises help bring tranquillity.

The Bajau peoples of South-East Asia, commonly called 'sea gypsies', have embraced this truth for centuries. They've had to – their livelihood relies on breath control. Traditionally, the Bajau have lived almost their entire lives aboard narrow lepa-lepa boats, free-diving to depths of thirty metres to spear fish and sea cucumbers or harvest clams and pearls.

There's no scuba gear or high-tech training involved, just a pair of homemade wood-and-glass goggles and the astonishing ability to hold their breath for up to five minutes. And this takes an incredible degree of composure.

Before a foray, each diver focuses all their energy on becoming completely relaxed and slowing their breathing, so that the heart-rate drops to about thirty beats per minute. Then they plunge.

While few of us will attain the near trance-like state that allows the Bajau to dive for so long, mastering the breath is within our grasp. Pranayama yoga, using principles of breath control, can facilitate a similar meditative state. Alternatively, simply find a quiet place, block out all distractions and focus solely on filling and emptying your lungs. Breathing is the most fundamental function of our being. Control it, and serenity is within your grasp.

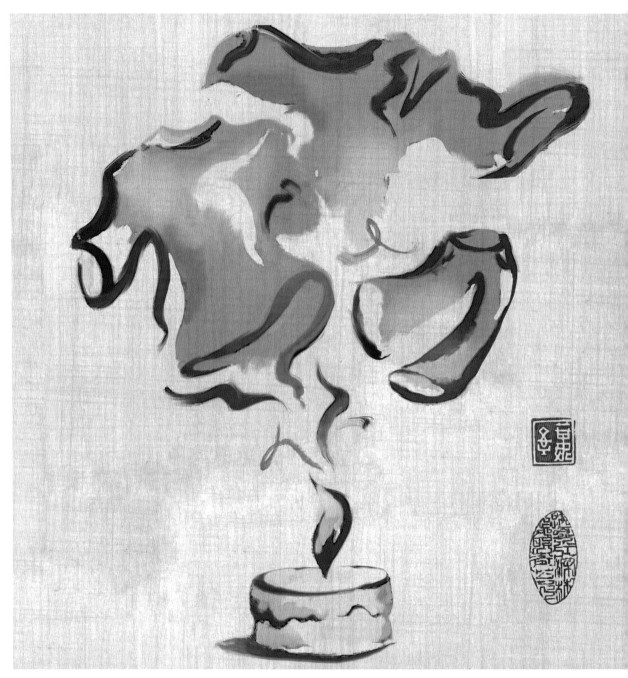

Soothing Scent

Secret Discover the power of aromatherapy

Tradition Burning incense **Date** Any time **Originated in** India, China and Japan

Olfaction is the first of our senses to mature. Our sense of smell is also profoundly sentimental. Odours, as distinct from visual messages, go straight to the brain's interpretive region where emotions are born and memories are stored. That's why smells are intimately entangled with feelings and recollections in ways not always easy to articulate. Furthermore, scent memory lasts longer than visual memory.

For thousands of years, the Chinese and Indians have used incense to uplift and heal.

Sandalwood sticks infuse the air at temples, purifying the mind for spiritual practice. Incense ingredients such as camphor, frankincense and star anise feature in traditional Chinese and Ayurvedic medicines as cures for nervous tension and respiratory ailments. The Japanese scent kimonos by hanging them over burners that are then filled with smouldering clove and turmeric. In the Chinese scholar's residence, agarwood wafts from the glowing tip of a coil, while its owner sits in meditative solitude.

After a long day, light a scented candle or incense stick in a darkened room or slide into a bath infused with essential oils. Inhale with eyes closed, letting lavender molecules nudge out all obsessivethoughts. Better still, hide the clock – Chinese monks once measured time with incense. The benefits of aromatherapy will give you renewed vigour to face the world.

Bath Bliss

Secret Soak your stresses away

Tradition Hot-stone bath **Date** Any time **Originated in** Bhutan

Known as a *dotsho* in the Dzongkha tongue, hot-stone baths are Bhutan's equivalent of Japan's *onsen*, Turkey's *hamman* and Scandinavia's sauna. Their history is sketchy but many believe the baths were originally the leisure activity of the well-to-do who devised ceremonies around the most auspicious dates for a ritualistic all-in soaking.

Cleansing the body and fending off the Himalayan cold were primary motivations, but the Bhutanese still believe the baths have medicinal benefits: healing minor skin problems, joint pains, arthritis and even diseases. The bath's natural elements of water, wood, fire, earth (the stones and leaves) and air also work together to induce mental and physical calm.

Whether indoors or alfresco, the ritual is the same. A wooden bath is filled with cool spring water. Rugby ball–sized white stones, hauled from local waterways, are heated red-hot in a wood fire, then tipped into the water. As they sizzle, bubble and steam, the water heats up. When they crack, therapeutic sulphuric minerals are released. Herbs and leaves are added to the water to aid healing, help moisturise the skin and release a natural aroma. The hotter the water the better, and a glowing brow is a sign that the treatment is expunging the body of its ills.

Now, more than ever before, the hot-stone bath is also about nurturing and pampering. Mimic the tradition at home with a steaming bath sprinkled with aromatic oils and bath salts. For a real natural-world immersion, try throwing in fresh rosemary leaves or lavender flowers straight from the garden.

Peace in Solitude
Secret Spend time alone

Tradition Poustinia (from the Russian for desert or solitary retreat)
Date Any time **Originated in** Russia

The nature of our world is that it keeps spinning. Life can feel like an endless treadmill of obligations from which we yearn to escape. What a privilege it would be to have some time to ourselves – quiet and alone – to really think, to listen to our hearts and, if it's our calling, to commune with the Almighty. Wouldn't this lead to profound serenity?

In the Russian Orthodox tradition, retreating to a *poustinia* plays just such a role. Usually a small, sparsely furnished cabin in the woods, the *poustinia* was traditionally the domain of a *poustinik*, a solitary, prayerful hermit. This was a place for silence, aloneness, inner contemplation and gaining wisdom. Today, while it's rare to find an ascetic *poustinik* living in full-time isolation, the concept of retreat to the *poustinia* is alive and well in Russia. From this and other traditions, it has spread around the world.

You don't have to become a hermit to experience the power of the *poustinia*. Make time, a day if you can, for solitude. Any place away from distraction and interruption will do. When you've spent some time in your own *poustinia* and experienced the insights it can bring, you might work towards attaining a '*poustinia* of the heart' – a silent, calm place to carry with you in the midst of a frenetic world.

Healing Waters

Secret Let water wash away your worries

Tradition River punting **Date** Any time **Originated in** England

The hushing breath of the sea, the trickle of a fountain, clouds mirrored in a pond – water is universally soothing to humans. Everyone from the fashion icon Diana Vreeland (who calls water 'God's tranquilliser') to the architects of the Ottoman empire recognises its refreshing and restful qualities. All over the world, from the Indian subcontinent to the Pacific islands, water is an essential element in rituals of cleansing and calming.

In the poem that begins Alice in Wonderland, Lewis Carroll describes a row along the river: 'All in the golden afternoon/full leisurely we glide ...'

Carroll, who was an Oxford don, beautifully evokes the dreamy pleasures of punting, a tradition at the great English universities. Drifting slowly with friends or sweethearts, stopping for a picnic under a willow tree, idling in the sunshine – what could be more deliciously peaceful?

Wherever you live, there's sure to be some water – a lake, stream, fishpond, even a fountain – that you can settle beside for an afternoon, perhaps with a cushion and a book, to feast your eyes and ears on the H_2O. Failing that, a bath, taken with no thoughts of haste or scrubbing, is the perfect way to slough off your cares.

Get Off the Grid

Secret Take a break from hyper-connectedness

Tradition Shabbat (Jewish day of rest) Date Sundown Friday to one hour after sundown Saturday Originated in Israel

Refraining from 'work' – defined by Jewish tradition as any effort to remake the world – is the heart and soul of Shabbat (the Sabbath). To create Shabbat *shalom* (Sabbath peace), observant Jews disengage from all the gadgets that make our twenty-first century hyper-connected, lives non-stop busy.

Telephones, internet, mobile phones, email, text messages, digital cameras, Twitter – for the duration of Shabbat all is powered down, unplugged and set aside. Life takes place not in the amorphous virtuality of cyberspace but locally, in the continuous present. Since there's no temptation to update faraway 'friends' or record things for posterity, what matters is the here and now: engaging with people who are actually present, opening up to the sublime beauty of the natural world, rediscovering the holiness and tranquillity that so often get brushed aside in the momentum of daily life.

If spending half the weekend off the grid seems a bit much, try creating your own regular 'gadget Sabbath'. One evening or weekend morning a week might work, or you could resolve to unplug whenever you spend romantic time with your partner or head to the park with your parents or kids. Even setting aside just a few distraction-free hours at the same time every week is an effective way to create a calm, rejuvenating space safe from electronic intrusions.

Nothing is Forever

Secret Embrace impermanence

Tradition *Dishu* (Chinese water calligraphy) **Date** Any time
Originated in China

Nothing lasts forever, so they say. But in many cultures, impermanence is celebrated rather than mourned. It helps us focus on what's really important in life.

According to Buddhist wisdom, attachment to impermanent things is the main cause of human suffering. Regardless of religious inclination, most people would agree that stressing over which smartphone to buy is detrimental to our spiritual wellbeing.

There are myriad ways to celebrate impermanence. In Tibet, Buddhist monks create and erase elaborate sand mandalas. In Thailand, temple visitors leave offerings of flowers as a reminder of the passing nature of material things.

The idea has modern resonance – in the 1990s, the newly invented art of water calligraphy swept across China. Today, millions of practitioners rise early each morning to paint intricate characters on roads and pavements using water instead of ink, leaving statements that are beautiful but temporary, destined to evaporate.

Apply the same thinking the next time you see condensation on a window. Use a finger to trace a word and watch the glass slowly cloud over, creating a new blank canvas. When you next go to the seaside, take a stick and leave a message in the sand, then watch as the tide sweeps the letters away. And muse on the idea that while the writing is temporary, the message is eternal.

Whipped to a State of Calm

Secret Feel the pain to achieve the pleasure

Tradition *Banya* (sauna) **Date** Any time **Originated in** Russia

Russians appreciate the cleansing, calming effects of regular trips to the *banya* (sauna) – even if some of the rituals appear to border on the sadomasochistic.

Start by shedding your clothes along with your inhibitions. On entering the *parilka* (steam room) wish your fellow bathers *Lyokogo* (pronounced lyokh-ka-va) *para!;* meaning something similar to May your steam be easy!

Using a long-handled ladle, toss some water on the furnace-heated rocks to release a burst of scalding steam into the room. A few drops of eucalyptus or pine oil (sometimes beer) can be added to the water to scent the steam.

Then stand up, grab hold of a *venik* (a tied bundle of birch branches) and beat yourself and/ or your fellow bathers. Following the birch-branch

thrashing – best experienced lying on a bench with someone else administering the 'beating'– run outside and plunge into the *basseyn* (ice-cold pool) or take a cold shower. The mild sting of the *venik* on your skin followed by the shock of the frigid water will soon be replaced by a sense of deep relaxation.

After repeating this process several times, finish by wishing your fellow bathers *S lyogkim parom!* (Hope your steam was easy!) and join them for a refreshing cup of tea sweetened with jam or herbs.

A similar experience can be achieved at home by combining a scalding hot bath with a vigorous, exfoliating skin scrub followed by a bracing cold shower. But the overriding lesson is that sometimes you need to take the pain before you can enjoy the bliss.

Turn up the Silence

Secret Find peace in quiet

Tradition Silent contemplation **Date** Any time
Originated in La Trappe Abbey, Normandy, France

Do you sometimes wish you could turn down the volume? Does the incessant chatter of daily existence leave you wishing for quiet? Silence offers space for listening to one's mind and creating calm, and yet real quiet is exceedingly rare.

For the Trappist order of Catholic monks and nuns, silence is a way of life. Trappists' monastic silence fosters mindfulness, solitude in community and openness to the spiritual. Of course, Trappists are not alone in their conviction that silence allows insights that the noisy world obscures. Religious traditions from Buddhism to Judaism to Zoroastrianism place value on quiet. In silence, one can access deep self-knowledge and more harmonious living.

You don't need to take a vow of silence to enjoy some quiet-induced calm. Just cut the volume in life's cacophony. Turn off the TV, unplug the music, unhook the phone – for an hour or an afternoon. There's no need to sit still, be alone or do nothing; Trappists work in quiet company. Just use the silence to really listen to your thoughts – and access this universal pathway to calm.

rhythm

Mantra Away the Madness

Secret Chanting stills the mind

Tradition Reciting mantras **Date** Any time **Originated in** India

We live in a mad world. An impatient world. A world constantly vying for the most precious real estate we own: our minds. From domestic demands to digital distractions, is it any wonder so many of us struggle to find space, inside our heads, for quiet contemplation?

Enter the mantra.

With its roots in India's ancient Vedic tradition, a mantra can be anything from a syllable to a sentence. The mantra has long been an integral component of Hinduism, with other faiths – such as Buddhism, Jainism and Sikhism – also embracing its basic tenets. The chanting of mantras is believed to deliver spiritual solace.

One of Hinduism's most propitious mantras is 'Om' (pronounced aum). Shaped like the number three in its written form, this tiny symbol represents mighty Hindu concepts – the creation, maintenance and destruction (in order for there to be renewal) of the universe. Both Hindus and Buddhists believe that, if intoned often enough with complete concentration, it leads to a state of blissful emptiness.

The beauty about mantras is you can recite them at any time, anywhere, in the privacy of your head. So, when you next find your mind swirling, switch off by switching inward and chanting a mantra. Whether it's the bite-sized meditative chant of Om, reciting your favourite song or even just slowly counting to ten, the key is to clear the clutter by focusing on an easily remembered sequence of sounds that works for you.

To Have and to Hold

Secret Reacquaint yourself with touch

Tradition *Kombolói* (worry beads) **Date** Any time **Originated in** Greece

Feeling overwhelmed by the hurly-burly of modern life with its incessant distractions and background noise? Now, imagine a Greek cafe full of senior gentlemen sitting contentedly all day, a study in serenity. They have an enviably unruffled aura, perhaps due to the idyllic Mediterranean vistas they gaze upon. In their hands they hold *kombolói* (worry beads), their fingers restlessly counting and flicking the beads.

Now, get a set of *kombolói* and remind yourself of the sense of touch.

In the increasing virtuality of modern life, we forget how things feel in our hands. The texture of olive wood or amber or glass beads across

the palm and the fingertips, or the clack-clack of flicking the beads are sensations to be savoured. Focusing on the sense of touch as you caress the beads allows a reconnection with the tangible, with the here and now.

Kombolói are similar to Turkish *tespih* (prayer beads) and to the Catholic rosary and *mala* in Buddhism. In Greece, however, they serve no religious function, but are merely a pleasant artefact to hold, to fidget with, to keep the hands occupied – thus avoiding lighting a cigarette.

In heightening the sense of touch, *kombolói* allow us to appreciate the tactile in an increasingly abstract world.

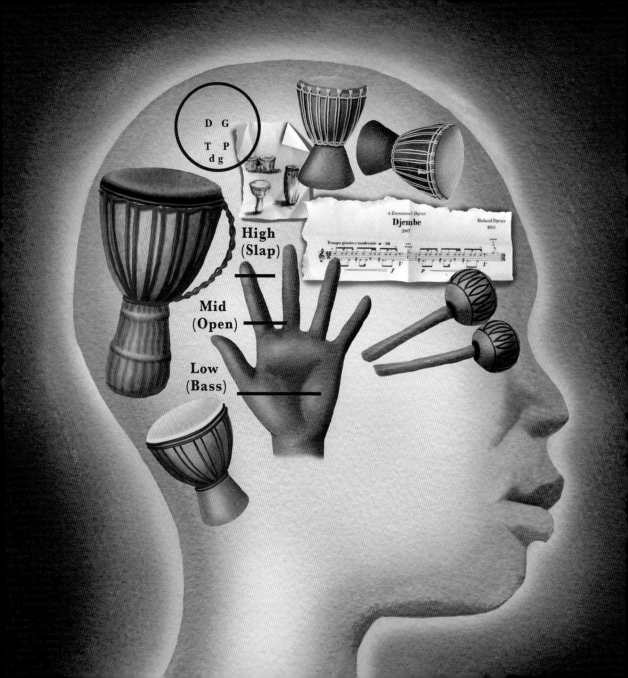

Feel the Beat

Secret Heal through rhythm

Tradition *Djembe* drumming **Date** Any time **Originated in** Mali

The world is a rhythmic place. The repetitive crashing of waves, the call of birds... Indeed, we start out in tune while still in the womb, hearing our mother's blood and the beat of her heart. In fact, the shushing sound humans around the world instinctively use to calm crying infants mimics those rhythms.

From shamans in native North American cultures to monks in Tibet to West African tribes, the drum has been a sacred object in almost every society on earth for millennia.

From low, thunderous bass notes to the bullwhip crack of a *djembe* 'slap', the complex instrument tells an emotional story with nary a word. In a drum circle, something magical happens; it's called *entrainment*. When our bodies collectively beat out the rhythm of nature, we connect with each other, with the planet, with the power of our own healing. In fact, *djembe* drumming has been proven to elicit theta brainwaves and altered states of consciousness, where drumming participants sense they've lost the isolating boundaries between themselves and the larger world.

So, do you have to fly to Mali or Senegal to experience this transformation? Not anymore. In the past few decades, *djembe* drumming's hypnotic quality has become popular throughout the Western world. You can't swing a dreadlock without hitting a drum circle in any town with even the faintest alternative culture. Or simply pop in a CD at home, feel the beat move you and transcend your own consciousness.

Born to Run

Secret Run for the pleasure of it

Tradition Distance running **Date** Any time
Originated in Sierra Madre region, Mexico

Ever dragged on your running shoes and forced yourself to take an uninspiring jog on a city footpath? Maybe you run from a sense of duty because you know running is good for you? You've heard about endorphins and the 'runner's high' so you know a good run will bring you calm. But why can't running be just a bit more enjoyable?

Ask a Tarahumara runner from the canyons and mountains of the Sierra Madre in Mexico about running as 'training' and they may look at you uncomprehendingly. For these remote living, indigenous people, running vast distances over tough terrain is a way of life as normal as sleeping and breathing. What's more, for the Tarahumara running is actually fun. The Tarahumara run to deliver messages, for transport between villages

and as part of a traditional ball game that goes on for days. With homemade tyre-tread sandals on their feet and joy in their hearts, they easily cover two hundred kilometres in a single run. And they finish smiling.

There's no need to run ultra-marathons to be like the Tarahumara. What we can learn from them, though, is to make running (or other regular exercise) a way of life and a pleasure, not a chore. Remember when you were a kid and wanted to run everywhere? Try to recapture this by exercising with a friend, listening to music or by jogging somewhere you can revel in nature. Whatever makes running a joy for you: do that. Your body – a natural running machine – will do the rest.

Tranquillity in a Tea Cup

Secret Slow down and appreciate simple rituals

Tradition Japanese tea ceremony
Date Throughout the year, with variances **Originated in** Japan

The Japanese tea ceremony, known as *chanoyu*, is a tradition with origins dating back more than one thousand years. The ritual has its roots in Zen Buddhism – green tea was brought to Japan from China by Buddhist monks in the ninth century and incorporated into meditation and other Buddhist practices. The tea ceremony that evolved has become an important custom in Japanese society and is revered as an art form and spiritual discipline.

The ceremony often takes place in a purpose-built tea room or teahouse, with the host serving *matcha* (powdered, green tea) to guests in graceful, choreographed movements. The central themes of the Way of Tea – harmony (*wa*), respect (*kei*), purity (*sei*) and tranquillity (*jaku*) – are evident as you sit quietly, enjoying your host's impeccable

hospitality and the simple act of drinking tea in austere yet elegant surroundings. The outside world and its clamour and chaos can be put aside; by focusing on the ritual and the serene, meditative atmosphere, you'll calm your mind and spirit. Achieving such mindfulness and paying attention to the here and now are central to the Zen Buddhist ideal of living in the present.

So if you're too caught up in your overscheduled lifestyle, your mind is a tempest of stress or you've forgotten to slow down and appreciate the simple things, why not include your own tea ceremony in daily life? Find a quiet space to sip a cuppa and just *be* in the moment. With a refreshed outlook you might come to realise that the thing worrying you was really just a storm in a tea cup.

Let Music Move You

Secret Harness the power of music

Tradition Gregorian chant **Date** Any time **Originated in** Italy and France

Cacophonous car alarms, screeching buses, competing televisions blaring 24-hour news… It's no wonder our modern acoustic plague has been implicated in everything from tinnitus to high blood pressure to heart disease.

Rewind a millennium or so. Imagine living in a mountaintop monastery in western or central Europe without the intrusion of a single artificial sound. Now, imagine creating a melodic, sacred music that brings listeners as close to the divine as your vocal cords allow.

While Christian sacred music has been around since New Testament days, Gregorian chanting took off in the ninth and tenth centuries. In fact, it became so popular that it spread to the farthest reaches of the known world and formed the basis of all Western music.

Brain-monitoring EEG machines have proven that Gregorian chanting can elicit greater alpha wave activity (what we create when we meditate). It can also decrease a holy trinity of modern ailments: blood pressure, elevated heart-rates and anxious thoughts.

Not heading to a monastic mountaintop? No matter, there are plenty of ways to achieve the same effects. As a mother of a newborn knows, any kind of gentle singing can instil wellbeing. And if Gregorian chanting isn't your style, find some other soothing music that speaks to you. Close your eyes, listen deeply and ride the waves of sound.

A Looming Peace

Secret Busy your hands to calm your mind

Tradition Weaving **Date** Any time **Originated in** Australia

A stressed mind feels like a big, tangled ball of yarn – snarled with worry and ugly loose ends. Unravelling this Gordian knot is no mean feat, and probing our problems can be like yanking on those dead-end threads that only pull the whole mess tighter.

When the mind can't solve our woes, it's helpful to turn to the body. The Dutch composer Simeon ten Holt famously said, 'My hands grasp at what my mind cannot "grasp": I believe in my hands.' The body has vast reserves of wisdom, and one way to tap into this is to set your hands a soothingly repetitive task.

Many of the Aboriginal peoples of Australia have weaving traditions that are still practised today.

Often the preserve of women, weaving can be used for practical purposes (for instance, to make baskets or sieves) or to make sacred objects for ceremonies. Traditionally, leaves and other plant fibres were used; in modern times, they have been supplemented by materials such as cane and string.

Complex tasks for the body still complex thoughts in the mind, and there's something immensely satisfying about seeing an object come to life in your hands through the steady collection of stitches. Even if you don't have the skill to whip up a hand-woven basket or an Argyle sweater, you can probably set yourself a bit of basic knitting – or play cat's cradle with your favourite pal in the sunshine.

回峰行

Exercise Your Demons

Secret When you're worked up, work out

Tradition *Kaihogyo* (physical endurance) **Date** Any time **Originated in** Japan

Anyone who has experienced the calm that comes from long-distance running will appreciate the core concepts of *kaihogyo*.

Followers of the Tendai sect of Buddhism believe that enlightenment can be achieved in the current life, and that the route to peace on earth is intense physical exertion.

To participate in the ritual of *kaihogyo*, novices must walk forty-two kilometres a day for one hundred days in the serene hills surrounding Mount Hiei. This entitles devotees to progress to the second stage – walking forty-two kilometres a day for another nine hundred days!

It should not be entirely surprising that since the Second World War, only thirteen monks have completed the *kaihogyo*.

Participants in the *kaihogyo* control their breathing as a way to controlling their minds. They complete circuits of the sacred mountain while reciting a repetitive mantra to eliminate mental distractions.

Next time you exercise, step up the intensity. Physical exertion encourages us to let go of everyday, humdrum distractions – did I water the plants or send that email? – and focus instead on the repetitive cycle of breathing. The exertion helps decrease stress hormones such as cortisol and increase endorphins, the chemicals that make us feel good.

You're unlikely to achieve enlightenment in one session, but you might be surprised by how relaxed you feel when you slip off your runners and return to your regular routine.

In a Spin

Secret Bring the ego into submission

Tradition *Sema* cermony of the whirling dervishes **Date** Any time
Originated in Konya, Turkey

Rotation is inherent in many things. Astronomers will tell you this, and so will the Sufi adherents of the Mevlevi order. Known as the whirling dervishes for their spinning dance, the Mevlevi aim to achieve mystical union with the Divine in their high-rotation *sema* ceremonies.

Revolving ceaselessly on their left feet, the whirling dervishes turn their right hands upwards and their left downwards, to connect heaven and earth. The *sema* becomes a mystical journey representing humankind's spiritual path through love to perfection.

For all their celestial aspirations, the Mevlevi are imbued with the imagery of death. Their black gowns indicate death, their tall caps a tombstone. The white robes that float around them as they whirl might look like an angel's wings but they represent funerary shrouds.

Yet such sombre overtones are a positive: they represent the death of the ego, an essential step on the path to enlightenment. By abandoning their egos, the whirlers can appreciate the oneness of all things and thus connect with the Divine.

While the whirling dervishes are a sect within Islam, their leader Cemaladdin Rumi welcomed all, whether wanderer, fire-worshipper or idolater.

If spinning like a dervish makes you giddy, remember it's just a tool to quell the ego. Find your own way to tranquillity by picturing yourself as a small part of a bigger whole. Overcoming desires relieves stress – it will get your head *out of* a spin – and reminds you of your connectedness with all creation.

Walk This Way

Secret Walking for walking's sake

Tradition Walking **Date** Any time **Originated in** Paris, France

There is a simple beauty in moving slowly across a landscape. Placing one foot in front of the other, unburdened by schedules, traffic, parking meters, obligations, plans, the mind is free to wander, to reflect, debrief, observe and discover, to delight in the things we routinely miss when hermetically sealed in metal containers flung around at in-human speeds. To walk is to move at the pace of our heartbeats, to hear the sound of our breath, to feel the strength of our muscles.

Though one of the first skills we acquire and an early milestone in our development, the concept of walking for pleasure is relatively recent. While ancient cultures (especially Cretan) walked labyrinths for meditative and religious purposes, it was the nineteenth-century poets such as Wordsworth, Thoreau and Baudelaire who kindled walking desire among the masses. In particular, Baudelaire extolled the *flâneur*, one who strolls with no objective other than to observe. Paris with its newly widened boulevards proved perfect for this pastime of ambulation and people-watching. The twentieth-century street photographers Doisneau and Cartier-Bresson owe much to this tradition.

You don't need an exotic location to be a *flâneur*. Rise early, walk out your front door, turn the corner and open yourself to the moment. Let fancy dictate your route, wander slowly, observe, explore and take random turns away from your cares. Use all your senses: smell, listen, touch, count the birds, smile, say hello to strangers; you'll find it's soothingly contagious.

sharing

Stop the Clock
Secret Take pleasure in waiting

Tradition Making *ataya* (West African 'gunpowder' tea)
Date Any time, preferably after sunset Originated in Senegal and the Gambia

All too often the Western mind struggles to let go of work, to choose an unfocused activity and to share such mellow moments with others. Perhaps the nearest many get to such conviviality is chatting idly in a pub or cafe. But if service is slow and you're waiting twenty minutes for your drink you're likely to get frustrated, and this valuable time is wasted.

But we don't necessarily have to succumb to annoyance. Indeed, in other cultures the shared anticipation of awaiting a drink can be as important as the drink itself. Such is the case of West African *ataya*.

Calling *ataya* 'tea' is about as inadequate as calling Guinness 'beer'. Served tequila-style in little glasses, *ataya's* intense sweetness cancels out a strident tannic bitterness to give a shot that is almost narcotic in its effect. As Gambian villages have no electricity, when the sun goes down the day's exhausting work must cease. Small groups of friends gather around a tiny, blue metal teapot, filled in almost equal measure with sugar, water and gunpowder tea-balls (Chinese green tea leaves hand-rolled into pellets). The mix is boiled and re-boiled, in between deft flourishes of accurate pouring from pot to glass, glass to glass, glass to pot in long, elegant streams. And all the while there's ample time to chat, smile and relish the evening calm.

So next time the coffee machine is taking a while to warm up, or the barman is having to change the barrels, why not savour the delay as a delightful opportunity for conversation and anticipation.

Let the Chips Fall

Secret Escape reality with play

Tradition Backgammon **Date** Any time **Originated in** Egypt

In a digital age it's all too easy to let every spare moment be gobbled up by smartphones and screens, but there are older, wiser ways to pass an idle moment.

In a slower time, people had to find amusements to see them through the long day. Games offer a perfect antidote to boredom, allowing players to enter a state where their minds are engaged but not stressed – something that repetitive email checking can't guarantee.

The ancient game of backgammon originated in the Middle East some five thousand years ago. Fragments of old boards have been unearthed in Iran, and stone *senet* boards (a predecessor to backgammon) have been uncovered in Egyptian tombs.

The tradition is still very much alive in Egypt. Even today, in many a Cairo cafe you will be able to find old men playing a leisurely game amid the fumes of the water pipes and the smell of sweet coffee.

Games that are often left behind in childhood can easily transport you back to that easy state of flow where you're absorbed in a task that is challenging (but not beyond your capabilities), yet pleasant so that time ceases to matter.

Backgammon, chess, Chinese chequers – any game you prefer will do – as long as it facilitates a gently stimulating escape from everyday concerns. And if you can find a congenially formidable opponent, all the better.

Stomp Out Your Stress

Secret Step in time with the crowd

Tradition *Dabke* folk dance **Date** Any time **Originated in** Lebanon

Banish the blues by sweating it out on the dance floor with your friends. The foot-stomping *dabke* is the strut-your-stuff stress remedy that doesn't require a prescription.

The folk dance is said to have originated in Lebanon's annual roof-rebuilding practice, back when the roofs were made from mud and straw. Once a year villagers would gather on top of each other's homes and, forming a line, shuffle across the roof, stamping in uniform rhythm to compact the dirt covering.

This communal synchronised stomping gradually made its way off the rafters and into the national culture, and today is performed throughout the Middle East in various forms. Just like its early roof-fixing beginnings, the *dabke* is a group activity. Everyone is invited to link arms and join the dance line, merrily stamping their way across the floor. Although it is traditionally performed at weddings and other celebratory occasions, in Lebanon it is just as common to see a spontaneous *dabke* take over the dance floor late at night in a bar.

Getting your groove on is a fail-safe way to lift your mood and restore tranquillity. Next time you feel the pressure start to build, grab your friends for some spur-of-the-moment dancing. A good foot-kicking boogie is sure to set your antenna back to calm.

The Magic of Touch
Secret Hold your loved ones close

Tradition Baby-wearing **Date** Every day
Originated in The Kalahari region of Botswana, Namibia and Angola

All cultures have their time-tested methods for calming fussy infants. But a tribe in southern Africa (the !Kung San tribe of the Kalahari desert) has mastered a series of techniques that would make any Western child psychologist jealous.

From birth through to the late toddler years, !Kung babies are rarely physically separated from their mothers. During the day they are carried close to the chest in a leather sling, breastfeeding regularly. The babies interact with their mothers more than Western babies do, but the mothers have both arms free to go about their day. While Western parents may consider it coddling, !Kung parents strive to meet all their babies' needs as quickly as possible.

As a result, ninety percent of !Kung parents can get their babies to stop crying within thirty seconds, and colic is virtually non-existent. When word got out, mothers and fathers around the world started holding their babies a little closer. The !Kung understand the deep calming qualities of human contact.

Make sure to spend time with your loved ones and hug them often, whether they are children, parents, partners or friends. They form your steady foundations in an unstable world. Embrace the lesson of the !Kung and reach out.

Destroy Your Anxieties

Secret Release your sadness and pain

Tradition The burning of Zozobra Date The second week of September
Originated in Santa Fe, New Mexico, USA

Each September in Santa Fe residents celebrate the Fiestas de Santa Fe, a festive commemoration of the Spanish retaking of the city in 1692. Since the 1920s, the highlight of this week-long celebration has been the burning of Zozobra, a massive, evil-looking marionette nicknamed Old Man Gloom.

The word *zozobra* means anxiety or anguish in Spanish, and the purpose of burning the Zozobra marionette is to symbolically destroy the anxieties and anguishes of the past year. Santa Feans write their worries on slips of paper and deliver them to the office of the local newspaper. These papers, which also include unpleasant legal documents such as divorce agreements or medical bills, are put in a special box and burned

along with Zozobra before a cheering crowd. As the marionette collapses into ash and cinders, spectators are released from their pain and given a fresh start.

You don't need to burn a fifteen-metre-high Zozobra to symbolically relinquish painful memories and anxieties. Throw a bonfire party and invite friends to toss papers expressing their worries into the flames. Or, for a slightly less dramatic cleansing, give your home a thorough once-over and trash anything negative – old love letters from bad exes, pink slips, clothes that no longer fit. When you're done, pop open a bottle of champagne and toast your newfound sense of lightness and peace.

A Package of Love

Secret Care for others

Tradition Making tamales Date Any time Originated in Mexico

In Náhuatl, the language of the Aztecs, *tamal* means wrapped, which perfectly describes this tasty Mexican dish – a steamed corn dough filled with a pick-and-mix combo of meat, vegetables, cheese, fruit or chillies, enveloped in a banana or corn leaf. For millennia Mexicans have believed that if you make tamales with bitterness or ill feeling, the disturbance in your heart will affect the flavour of the tamales. (This tradition is at the heart of the Mexican book and film *Like Water for Chocolate*.) Instead, as you fold up the green packages, think fondly of the loved ones who will enjoy unwrapping and biting into these crumbly, warm gifts.

It is easy to get wrapped up in your own stress, but caring for others can be calming. To know that somebody else is healthier and happier because of you gives you a sense of purpose and control. You realise that you have the ability to manage your own worries. It also shifts your internal focus and silences those troubling thoughts shouting for attention.

You don't need to make an elaborate meal to achieve this calm; caring can be as simple as visiting a sick friend, complimenting a stranger or doing a favour for someone in need. If you do decide to feed someone, perhaps consider a package of tamale love.

Coal, Calm and Collected

Secret Share your load

Tradition Spanish firewalking **Date** Midnight on Midsumer's Eve (23 June)
Originated in San Pedro Manrique, Castile, Spain

Humans are social creatures, so when problems weigh on our shoulders we seek support from loved ones. Having another point of view helps us find a way out of circular worries, or makes us see that the problem is more of a candle flame than an inferno. Likewise, helping others with their woes distracts us from our own problems and often puts our concerns into perspective.

In many cultures, walking barefoot over hot coals is a shared test of adversity. In San Pedro Manrique in northern Spain, crowds gather to watch men carry somebody on their backs in the *paso del fuego* (firewalking). The trick to avoiding burnt pinkies is that taking the weight of another avoids combustion.

The firewalking pair stares down the red-hot wood embers, the drums beat and the crowd in the square looks on. Then something remarkable happens: the heartbeats of both participants and observers thump in unison. There is a group trance-like calm, everyone sharing the adversity ahead.

Stomping over barbecue coals in the backyard isn't the best path to calm. Instead, chat with a friend about what's heavy on your mind. This doesn't mean complaining or being a burden, but valuing their opinion and letting them express their friendship. Even speaking to a stranger with no vested interest can cool your anxiety and make you feel you aren't alone.

Unity in a Bowl

Honour friendship over a drink

These days, eating and drinking is often a solo, distracted activity. We absentmindedly snack in front of the television or down an energy drink on our way to the gym.

Now, imagine the opposite – taking hours to revere the process, to honour your elders and hosts, or to appreciate the life-enhancing properties of both sustenance and our interconnectedness.

If you visit the South Pacific, you might find yourself invited to a kava ceremony, a common occurrence in cultures where gift-giving and hospitality are an integral part of society. The ceremonies are not so much about kava itself – although the sedative and intoxicating qualities of the beverage certainly help foster relaxation and sociability – but about the sacredness of our connections. Often, the drink is poured into a communal kava bowl and emptied by each participant before being refilled and passed on. The ceremony might be religious or political, or a social event with storytelling, but the feeling of unity and community is the same.

Not heading to Polynesia next week? *A`ole pilikia*, or no worries, as they'd say in Hawaii. Although you can find kava (also known as kava kava) in capsule or tea form in many Western countries, you can recreate the important aspects of the kava ceremony without the kava. Do you grab a drink with friends at the pub every Friday night? Try adding a toast to your friendship first. Sit back, smile at the connections you've created and drink it all in.

A Problem Shared is a Problem Halved

Secret Discuss your thoughts and fears

Tradition Dream-sharing Date Any time Originated in Ecuador

Have you ever woken up with a start and spent a whole day disturbed by a nightmare? Or perhaps you've dreamed something wonderful, which you fervently hope might come true. Perhaps you've wondered about the meaning of dreams and tried to interpret their subconscious worlds. If you knew the deepest fears and dreams of those you lived with, wouldn't you gain a window to their souls?

Each morning before dawn, Achuar families in the Amazon forests of Ecuador gather to drink tea and share their dreams. This ritual creates a strong bond between extended family members in these close-knit communities, and the content of dreams determines much about the day's activities. For the Achuar, dream-sharing is like peering deep into the psyches of those they live with; it fosters mutual understanding, creates community cohesion, encourages consideration of others' viewpoints and, ultimately, it brings peace.

If you want to bring more calm and cohesion to your family or your community, revealing the depths of your mind might be a useful place to start. You don't need to get up in the pre-dawn dark and conduct a formal discussion of your mind's night-time wanderings, but do take time to get to the core of things. Share your thoughts, fears and nightmares with those closest to you and allow them to do the same. When you have nothing to hide you create a more harmonious you, a more trusting community and, just maybe, a better world.

Pressing the Flesh

Secret Accept the human touch

Tradition *Lomi lomi* massage Date Any time Originated in Hawaii, USA

Touch is a basic human need, as vital to our wellbeing as food and warmth. There is even evidence to suggest that touch is essential to cognitive development in infants. As adults, if we're lucky, our tactile needs are taken care of by friends, family and lovers, but it can still do us a world of good to pay special attention to our physical selves.

Getting – or giving – a massage is the perfect way to reconnect with the body and to discover the blissful ways touch can release the knots in both muscles and mind.

Massage is a revered art in many traditional cultures. In Hawaii, *lomi lomi* massage is a practice hundreds of years old, enriched by a spiritual philosophy that seeks to unite the individual soul with the infinite. It is characterised by rhythmic movements, often performed with the whole arm, which evoke the ebb and flow of waves. The ultimate way to have *lomi lomi* is from two masseurs working in harmony. You're practically guaranteed an immersive experience that will take you out of the quotidian realm and into a synapse-soothing trance.

If you can't find a *lomi lomi* practitioner near you, there are plenty of other forms of massage that will work the tranquillity trick – or you could try doing a course with a friend. That way, you'll both have rejuvenating touch on tap.

Laugh in the Face of Danger

Secret Make fun of your fears

Tradition Halloween Date 31 October Originated in United Kingdom

Think positive and all will be okay, right? Sometimes this advice can backfire – insisting that things will be great can make it seem terrible if the situation sours.

The Stoic philosophers of ancient Greece had a different approach to managing anxiety. They believed in pondering the worst-case scenario with a sober mind, fleshing out their anxiety with details and parameters. With every angle considered, anxiety over the ifs and maybes gave way to calm.

For example, Seneca the Stoic suggested that a person who is afraid of losing their wealth should set aside a few days to live roughly and cheaply, and to ask themselves if such an outcome is so bad after all. Similarly, Halloween lets us laugh in the face of our anxieties about death, the abject and the demons that spook us. It's also an excuse to become somebody else for a night.

Halloween is thought to have begun as the Pagan festival Samhain, where people wore costumes to disguise themselves while warding off ghosts. Trick-or-treating started out in Great Britain and Ireland with children and the poor singing and reciting prayers for the dead at people's doorsteps in return for cakes. It is now very popular in the United States and Canada.

You can't dress up as the undead every day of the week but you can list your anxieties and how you would handle your worst-case scenarios. Imagine that you are reading the list months after the outcome and laughing at your anticipated fears. It's worth a try. What's the worst that could happen?

Be Here Now

Secret Stay in the present

Tradition The Pirahã language **Date** Any time
Originated in Amazon jungle, Brazil

The Pirahã people of Brazil, just a few hundred strong, live a life of startling simplicity along the verdant banks of the Maicí River, a tributary of the Amazon. There, they maintain their traditional lifestyle and unique language, despite decades of contact with Western culture.

One of the keys to their fierce independence and powerful sense of identity is their commitment to the now – so profound that it's embedded in their language. According to Daniel Everett, an authority on the Pirahã language and culture, the Pirahã people believe that only observable experience is real and worth talking about, so they don't talk in abstractions much; in fact, their grammar, with its lack of tenses, doesn't permit it.

Instead of dwelling on a past nobody can recall, discussing people that haven't been met or disputing the existence of gods nobody has seen, they sit on the banks of their river, chatting about concrete everyday matters. It might sound mundane to some, but anyone lucky enough to meet the Pirahã can't help but notice the amount of laughter and affection embedded in their conversation.

It's a shame the language is so obscure as it might contain some keys to human happiness. But we can still be inspired by their example and stop obsessing about the long-since-past and the yet-to-be. Only the present is real, so grab hold of it and enjoy it before it vanishes.

Pause for Thought

Secret Enjoy just being

Tradition *Keyif* (relaxation) Date Any time Originated in Turkey

Roughly translated, the Turkish word *keyif* means relaxation. It sums up an important part of the Turks' steady approach to life – namely, taking the time, at least once a day, to simply stop, sit down and recharge. You don't have to be Turkish to know that the best way to do this is over a hot drink, and Turks frequent *çay bahçesi* (tea gardens) and *kahvehanes* (coffee houses) for restorative *keyif* sessions.

In its classic form, *keyif* involves a few important props. There's the *çay* (tea) of course, typically served black, in a tulip-shaped glass and sweetened with numerous sugar cubes. Less potent *elma* (apple) tea and tar-like *Türk kahve* (Turkish coffee) are also on offer. Turks who want to seriously unwind and socialise – all while their brain subconsciously solves problems – incorporate a game of backgammon and a

nargile (water pipe) stuffed with sweet-smelling apple tobacco.

This beloved ritual of pausing to exchange gossip or just quietly reflect has spawned numerous local customs and proverbs. The traditional Turkish saying, 'A cup of coffee commits one to forty years of friendship' summarises the camaraderie that accompanies a shared cuppa. At the end of a cup of Turkish coffee, drinkers tip the sludgy residue into the saucer and read their friend's fortune in the patterns.

Luckily, you don't have to be in a spice-scented bazaar to enjoy the morale-boosting effects of slowing down and appreciating the moment while catching up with friends and, most importantly, yourself. Try it with English tea, biscuits and the crossword; it's just as effective.

Put Your Best Face Forward

Secret Be someone else for a while

Tradition Masquerade ball **Date** Ten days leading up to Shrove Tuesday
Originated in Venice, Italy

Sometimes we just want a break from ourselves, to see the world through another pair of eyes. By stepping into somebody else's life, our own problems fade away. The act of donning a mask gives us permission to express our wilder, more sophisticated, or calmer, side.

Masquerade balls became popular among the upper classes of Venice in the sixteenth century. Venice was a socially oppressive place with narrow streets, offering little privacy. During Carnivale, *signores* and *signoritas* concealed their identities and social standing behind costumes and simple masks of leather, porcelain and glass. This allowed them to flirt and associate with people of other classes without judgement. To preserve their anonymity, many men made themselves appear grotesque

by wearing the *bauta*, a caped disguise with a mask dominated by a large beak. The protrusions allowed them to eat and drink without revealing who they were.

Assuming another identity can free you up when you feel trapped. It creates distance between yourself and your worries, and helps put you at ease. If you can't take to the stage or a ballroom in character, you can certainly do so in your own mind. Think of someone who'd stay calm in your situation. What would they say? How would they move? Wear something different to break the routine and get into the persona. Acting like somebody at ease can trick a jittery headspace into feeling calm. Glide through your day with a royal, graceful demeanour and your body will tranquilly follow.

Speak Your Truth

Secret Don't bottle it up

Tradition Sharing circles Date Any time Originated in North America

Negative feelings can rattle even the most Zen-like among us. Anger, disagreement, a sense that we've been treated unfairly – all constitute the range of emotions that make us human. It's what we do with less-than-positive thoughts that determine the difference between stress and serenity.

Indigenous tribes in North America have an ancient oral tradition that helps people express what's on their mind: the sharing circle. In aboriginal cultures the circle is an important symbol of unity and connectedness. When people gather in this formation everyone is equal and no-one dominates, nobody exists in isolation. A talking stick is passed around the circle from person to person, marking the opportunity for each to speak freely and honestly while everyone respectfully receives their words. The simple technique has been used to voice opinions and concerns, defuse and manage conflict and even help heal after traumatic events.

Sharing circles are increasingly recognised by educators, therapists and organisational experts as a communications tool that honours individuals and facilitates a sense of calm.

The approach can be useful for family or workplace issues, but the concept of finding our voice can be used by anyone, at any time. Particularly when an internal storm is brewing, it's important not to keep it all inside. Speaking up prevents unexpressed feelings from festering and creating further discord. You can spread the serenity by encouraging others to speak up, too.

Shop Your Way to Zen

Secret Indulge in retail therapy

Tradition The Great Singapore Sale **Date** Late May to late July
Originated in Singapore

Shopping is a necessity for many of us, whether we like it or not. Groceries, clothes, household items: nary a week (or a day for some!) goes by when we don't pull out our wallets. As commonplace as shopping is, Singaporeans have managed to transform what could be a stressful experience into something altogether different.

Singaporeans have perfected the art of shopping in a city that's packed with shopping-crazy denizens. Glittering megamalls provide an airconditioned escape for the masses, offering restaurants, cinemas and other entertainment, special shopping fairs and freebies galore. This retail therapy reaches its zenith in the annual two-month-long Great Singapore Sale, a nationwide shopping extravaganza that attracts visitors from around the world.

With almost every store on the island promoting massive discounts, it's almost Grand Central Station at rush hour all day, every day. To outsiders, the scene seems incomprehensible. Yet locals have learnt to embrace the queues and the crowds with a Zen-like mentality. In a place where waiting in line is the norm, patience in pursuit of a bargain is a virtue borne of necessity.

It's no wonder the crowds gather. There is a certain pleasure derived from shopping. Finding a rare vintage Beatles LP at a thrift store, rewarding yourself with a new dress, ticking off your Christmas list early or just spending a few hours away from the worries of life can really lift your mood. Just be careful not to turn retail therapy into a black hole of credit-card debt.

Unburden Yourself

Externalise your worries

Tradition Worry Dolls **Date** Any time **Originated in** Guatemala

An overflowing inbox or never-ending to-do list – when your head is swirling with stuff, it's difficult to calm your mind. With so much to think about in our complex and demanding lives, it's no wonder anxiety is on the rise. But fretting about things impairs your ability to get things done and can disrupt your sleep, raising stress levels even higher.

Worry not. There are ways to dispense with disruptive thoughts and maintain your equanimity. Take a lesson from Guatemala. Legend has it that when a pair of native Mayan children was overcome with worry over family problems, they fashioned a family of tiny, colourful dolls to whom they told their concerns.

Placing these 'worry dolls' beneath their pillows, the children drifted into a peaceful slumber and woke up feeling refreshed and inspired to overcome their challenges. The dolls had taken their worries away!

Grown-ups can also banish harried thoughts by releasing them from the confines of the mind. Talk to a friend when things have got you in a tizzy, or write down your concerns on a piece of paper. Articulating your worries is the first step towards reducing emotional turmoil and gaining control. The freed-up energy will not only allow you to craft solutions, you'll discover a much clearer headspace.

Dance into the Unknown

Secret Surrender control

Tradition The tango **Date** Any time **Originated in** Buenos Aires, Argentina

On any night of the week in Buenos Aires, you can head to a *milonga* (a place where tango is danced) and dance into the wee hours.

It could be a small, musty bar on a cobbled back street or alternatively a glittering nineteenth-century salon on one of the city's elegant avenues; wherever you go you'll find dozens of women in terrifyingly high heels dancing backwards to the melancholy strains of the *bandoneón*; eyes closed, an expression of sheer bliss and peace on their faces.

The tango's steps aren't set in stone. The female dancer doesn't know what's coming next, or what's behind her. She is defenceless in the face of a sharp left kick from a set of stilettos to her starboard side, but if she's captained by a skilful and considerate partner, she's safe.

Dancing backwards requires a degree of surrender we're not used to. It can induce panic at first, but with practice it can become a beautiful, transporting and calmly exciting experience.

The gender politics might sound antifeminist, and maybe they are, but this is the dance floor; it's not real life. These days men, too, can experience this blissful surrender at any number of edgier *milongas* where role-swapping is part of the fun.

So whenever you find yourself facing something new and intimidating, be inspired by the tango: close your eyes, smile, trust in those around you and take the first step.

focus

Take Aim at a Single Target

Secret Focus on one aim and eliminate distractions

Tradition Archery **Date** Any time, especially weekends and during *tsechus* (festivals) **Originated in** Bhutan

On the face of it, an archery contest in Bhutan seems an unlikely paragon of calm. Whether the competition involves a few friends gathered on a Saturday morning or one of the regular regional tournaments, you can expect barracking of ear-splitting volume and ribaldry.

Although archery is essentially a martial sport, here it's definitely not about killing. In this staunchly Buddhist Himalayan kingdom, bows and arrows are used for hitting targets, not for harming living beings. Still, archery (*datse* in the Dzongkha language) is considered a measure of manliness, hence loudly insulting your rivals is all part of the game, and banks of cheerleaders sing lewd ditties to distract each archer's attention from the distant and diminutive mark.

And therein lies the lesson. Hitting the centre of a small, wooden target 140 metres away, particularly with a traditional bamboo bow, doesn't only require physical prowess, technical ability and clear eyesight. It also demands the ability to shut out the jeering and heckling of adversaries, and the singing and gesticulations of your opponents' cheerleaders.

Try picking up a bow and arrow yourself at an archery range. Block out the distractions of sight and sound. Hone your focus so that all else fades away except those concentric yellow, red and blue circles. Whether you hit the bull's eye or not doesn't really matter. Training your senses to converge on that single, distant point is an effective way to attain absolute calm.

Clear the Clutter

Secret Create order in your environment

Tradition Feng shui Date Any time Originated in China

It's often said that our external world reflects our inner world. With this in mind, take a look at your home and office. Are you living and working in an oasis of calm? Or do your daily environments resemble a cyclone zone? Regardless of how your surroundings measure up, consider that your living and working quarters may affect your state of mind. A cluttered environment can increase stress and breed chaos and procrastination. An ordered environment, on the other hand, often facilitates efficiency.

In China, the belief that environment affects a person's wellbeing is a cornerstone of the more than four-thousand-year-old practice of feng shui, often known as the art of placement. Commonly applied to interior design, feng shui uses techniques such as clearing excess material objects, specific furniture arrangements and intentional colour choices to optimise the flow of *chi*, or universal energy, thereby enhancing wellbeing. Trained practitioners assess the flow of *chi* throughout a structure, removing elements that create disharmony, distress and stagnation in a person's life. Good feng shui puts you and your surroundings in balance, better able to receive the gifts of the universe.

Even if you don't embrace the belief system, applying some basic principles can help create serenity. Light blue, for example, evokes a sense of calm and is ideal in bedrooms. And who can argue against cleaning up clutter? Eliminate frenzied searches for things and your days will undoubtedly sail along more smoothly.

KEEP CALM AND DRINK TEA

Down to a Tea

Secret Observe the niceties

Tradition High tea **Date** Every afternoon **Originated in** Great Britain

Wherever you are, try this: at the stroke of the next hour, stop. Whatever you're working on, just stop.

Next: become British.

Finished? Good.

Now, sit down for thirty minutes. Reach for your culture's iconic symbol, which has been synonymous with relaxation and refinement for almost two hundred years. Following established protocol, go through a series of steps, carefully preparing said symbol for ingestion. If you'd like to honour friends with your hospitality, invite them over. Argue (politely!) about the appropriate time to pour the milk. Then, drink it in. Breathe in the familiar aroma. Normal life will start again soo—. Wait, never mind. Worry about that later. It's tea time.

The ceremony of drinking afternoon tea dates back to the 1840s, and the ritual quickly became a British tradition. Wherever there were British subjects – at home, in a war-time factory, in a posh hotel at the far reaches of the Empire – they would stop time as their mother's mother did and their children's children would do. While afternoon tea now ranges from a single cuppa to the traditional high tea – teapot, dainty sandwiches with the crusts removed, scones or other sweets – what remains is the familiar, comforting structure of the event.

So next time you break for tea (or your chosen beverage), don't rush through it, tossing back a hastily prepared brew before getting back to more pressing things. Take the time to do it properly. Get out the good china, allow yourself a sweet treat and appreciate a moment of luxury. Jolly good, I hear you say!

Good Things Come to Those Who Wait

Secret Practice patience

Tradition Stilt fishing **Date** April to October **Originated in** Sri Lanka

Speed-dating. Quick fix. Same-day shipping. Fast food. Fast credit. Fast track. We live in an age of instant gratification where delay is akin to death and the only answer to 'When do you want it?' is 'Five minutes ago'. But impatience has never been a virtue, and eye-rolling and foot-stamping don't lead to peacefulness. Whatever happened to the value of waiting?

Forbearance is a way of life for the stilt fishermen of Sri Lanka; indeed, their livelihood depends on it. Stilt fishing, native to the country's south-west, involves teetering precariously on a small crossbar (called a *petta*) atop wobbly, two-metre stilts fixed into the sea bed, and waiting for a bite. And then waiting some more. While modern fishing methods are, of course, available, the anglers have forgone progress for the past, renouncing noisy boat engines for their unobtrusive poles, and casting lines rather than nets so as not to scare off their precious quarry. Stilt fishing can be gruelling and time-consuming but it offers rich rewards, usually in the form of a juicy mackerel or spotted herring.

We can't all sail off to Sri Lanka and perch atop poles in a quest for quietude. But it's easy enough to discover the payoffs of patience in our own hectic lives. Swear off the supermarket and grow your own vegetables or herbs, bake a complicated cake, write a love letter and watch the postbox for a reply. Or grab your own fishing rod, head downriver and wait. And then wait some more.

the first of here
be from Saint
?ements on the
to come up and
will for I had
?ell and water
the edge of
the gates were

?ind the fruit
?d had the best
? all the south
? great barrels
? making a
?rough he would
?d acknowledge it.

July 21st

This morning, I harvested the wheat in the south field. The yield was not so good this year, owing to the dry weather in the last few months. Later I travelled by train to Dabble creek where a great many houses were burned last year in the fall. The Eastern settlement was badly affected and I went to offer our help with some of the rebuilding. It will be many more months before the town is on its feet again. It made my heart ache to travel through country that once was thriving and more than used

3rd · SINGLE SINGLE · 3rd
Eastern Avenue Passenger Railway Co.
EXCHANGE TICKET
8 Cts. This ticket, being issued at a reduced price, is only good for This Day for a Continuous Ride from Junctions of Roads names, and is NOT TRANSFERABLE. [OVER]

Express it on Paper

Secret Record your feelings

Tradition Mormon journal-keeping **Date** Any time **Originated in** USA

Members of the Church of Jesus Christ of Latter-day Saints, also known as Mormons, are champion journal-keepers. From an early age, all Mormons are encouraged to write regularly, and Mormon children often receive hardbound journals for birthday or Christmas presents. The origin of this tradition is rooted in biblical passages about the importance of record-keeping, but modern church leaders speak of journaling as a way for church members to reflect on their faith, their lives, their problems and their joys.

There's plenty of non-religious evidence that journaling helps us to feel happier, calmer and less stressed. Psychology research shows that journaling reduces the intensity of negative emotions, helps us solve problems more critically and clarifies confusing feelings. Regular journaling has even been shown to strengthen immune cells and decrease the symptoms of asthma, arthritis and other painful conditions. The process of expressing your feelings in writing helps you release unpleasant thoughts and gain a clearer perspective and sense of control.

To achieve the calming benefits of journaling, commit to writing regularly. Whether this is once a day or once a week, it doesn't matter as long as you stick to your schedule. Find a quiet place to write – your bedroom, your backyard, a peaceful cafe – and just allow your thoughts to pour out. You're guaranteed to feel more relaxed and upbeat when you finally put down your pen.

The Road Ahead

Secret Focus on the journey, not the destination

Tradition Walking the Shikoku Pilgrimage **Date** Any time, though traditionally undertaken in spring or autumn **Originated in** Shikoku, Japan

Increasingly, we're obsessed with reaching our destinations as quickly as possible. We fly, we take the fastest train and program our sat-nav to calculate the shortest possible route.

Pilgrimages represent a very different kind of travel. Though most have a specific goal – a saint's birthplace, holy mountain or sacred shrine – the real virtue is in the effort of the journey. And the Shikoku Pilgrimage is different again: not only is the destination beside the point, there is no destination.

Since the ninth century, *henro-san* (pilgrims), devotees of the Shingon Buddhist saint Kōbō Daishi, have walked a one-thousand-kilometre circuit around the island of Shikoku, visiting eighty-eight temples en route. You can start and finish at any one; the circle will still be complete.

In detaching from the hustle and (in Japan, intense) bustle of everyday life and entrusting themselves to the care of Kōbō Daishi, pilgrims progress through four spiritual stages, from awakening faith to enlightenment and nirvana. After a month or two of walking in a circle, serenity is embedded in the soul.

To discover the peace that travelling without a destination brings, simply take a walk from where you are, and back again. Don't think about where you're headed, simply focus on what you're seeing, hearing and smelling at any given moment, and on the sensation of your feet moving one in front of the other. Now, that's a reliable road-map to calm.

Be Prepared

Order is the enemy of chaos

Tradition *Mise en place* (to put in place) **Date** Any time **Originated in** France

Even the best of us can be driven insane by coming close to finishing a task, only to realise a forgotten critical step that requires us to start again from scratch. Preparation is the key to success as there is no better way to put a distracted mind at ease than a sense of order.

An obligatory lesson for any professional chef in training, the French term *mise en place* refers to the practice of ensuring ingredients and equipment are prepared and assembled as required, ready for the food to be cooked and served. The process is critical to the efficient and smooth running of a restaurant, which might need to serve hundreds of meals or satisfy the time-critical demands of hungry customers. Stellar chefs appreciate the importance of each task required to create a majestic wedding cake, a humble minestrone or a twice-baked soufflé.

At home, a little *mise en place* could make the family meal less chaotic, a languishing project that much more achievable and a repetitive chore a little less tedious. Take the time to think about and focus on the process of preparation and organisation. It's sure to lead to a far more relaxing experience and can be just as rewarding as reaching the end goal.

Walking the Tightrope

Secret Balance body, mind and soul

Tradition Slacklining **Date** Any time **Originated in** California, USA

According to the principles of yoga, longevity is more than just a long life. It is also the complete balance of body, mind and soul. In yoga, finding equilibrium in our lives brings the health and happiness that can make life not just longer, but better.

Rock-climbers unwittingly put these principles into practice when they started slacklining three decades ago in Yosemite National Park. Looking for ways to improve their balance in between ascents, they turned the tubular webbing commonly used in climbing into tightropes. What started as walking led to jumping, flipping and fluid sequences of yoga poses – all while balanced on a one-inch-wide line.

Nowadays, wherever there are climbers, surfers or snowboarders around, you'll find a slackline swaying between two trees.

Learning to balance on a slackline is a practice of moving meditation that requires total focus. Staying balanced while moving through a sun salutation puts you in the zone, a bliss state known in yoga terms as *samadhi*, where all the worries of the world disappear. You focus instead on your flailing arms, the tightness of your jaw and the clenching in your stomach and, over time, discover how all that tension is holding you back. Eventually, you learn to focus on simply balancing.

Balance is the key to longevity or, in slackline terms, avoiding a face-plant. One trick is to find a *dristi*, a fixed point in the distance to focus on. Another is to breathe, even when you are feeling your most challenged.

Regardless of whether you're standing on a slackline, try using these techniques to find balance and focus in your day-to-day life.

Aim for Excellence

Secret Become an expert in your chosen area

Tradition Japanese specialty restaurants **Date** Any time **Originated in** Japan

Getting caught up in life's rat-race means we constantly aspire to be the best at everything and anything. Often, however, we can become disillusioned when faced with the disappointing reality of being mediocre at too many tasks. Mastering a specific skill helps to soothe and de-clutter the mind by reducing complexity and forcing us to focus on a single objective.

At specialty restaurants in Japan, chefs devote their lives to the mastery of their chosen dish so that a customer can experience the finest and fullest expression of a particular food at the peak of its season – the freshest sushi, the most tender chicken yakitori or the silkiest tofu. It is even said that the ability to truly savour the lightest, crispiest tempura is only possible in a specialty restaurant where the food is deep-fried at the ideal temperature and quickly consumed on the spot. Sushi chefs, who famously train for many years to cook perfectly textured rice and source the best fish, are justly revered for their supreme dedication to their craft.

Repetition is easily dismissed as a trigger for boredom but the discipline of regularly invoking a familiar action can become a cherished and comforting ritual. Over time, the expertise acquired also gives us a sense of achievement from a job very well done.

Sweat the Small Stuff

Secret Concern yourself with the task at hand

Tradition Mushroom hunting **Date** Spring and autumn **Originated in** Russia

This is the multitask millennium. We blog as we work, walk as we text, tweet as we travel, lunch with one friend and message five others. The question is no longer 'to be or not to be', it is 'to be uploaded, shared, photographed, captioned and commented upon… or not to be at all'. In the race to be part of something big – to know everything, go everywhere, be connected to everyone – have we forgotten how to pay attention to detail?

The mushroom hunters of Russia haven't. For centuries, they've traipsed into the forest, eyes trained on the ground, searching for quarry. While mushrooms have sustained the Russian people in times of famine and are a staple of national cuisine, there's a fine line between the flavoursome and the fatal. Mushroom foraging is known in Russia as 'the quiet hunt' for very good reason: without serious contemplation, concentration and intense scrutiny, that bite of mushroom *pelmeni* (dumpling) could be a 'shroom-stalker's last.

While Russians from the wealthiest oligarch to the most bucolic babushka adore the thrill of the chase, it's the engrossing nature of the search that instils a sense of calm. There can be no distractions when seeking out the most perfect – and least toxic – morsel.

This singleminded serenity can be learned by even the most fungiphobic. Set aside an hour or so – use a timer if it helps – to tackle a single task or simple meditation without digression. Then focus… as if your life depended on it.

Lighten Your Load

Secret You are more than your possessions

Tradition Aboriginal culture **Date** Any time **Originated in** Australia

The diverse tribes and nations that constitute Aboriginal society have some important things in common – but 'things' aren't one of them.

The first Australians share a way of life that is concerned with cultural enrichment, amassing more than forty thousand years' worth of stories, songs and rituals, rather than possessions.

To this day, status among Aboriginal people is based on a person's inner qualities and abilities. The elderly are particularly valued as repositories of the knowledge that lies at the heart of every person and within each tribe's sense of identity and worth.

To be sure, the nomadic lifestyle isn't conducive to accumulating stuff, especially because the social structure is non-hierarchical and there are no slaves to cart the gear. But it goes beyond practicality. Aboriginal tradition places a marked emphasis on the value of cultural capital above the physical. In general, the few kept possessions were simple, elegant objects such as woven baskets, weapons and musical instruments.

Many of these possessions were valued as much for the stories they carried – the way fish traps were woven, the burnt markings on the didgeridoos and baby-carriers – as the things themselves.

So consider this philosophy when you survey your own possessions. Keep those that have real meaning and shed anything that is redundant. And remember: creating and enjoying beauty carries no requirement to possess it.

Keep Your Dreams Alive

Secret Affirm your hopes

Tradition Wishing tree **Date** Any time **Originated in** Turkey

When you feel burdened by all you wish to accomplish, it can be difficult to achieve serenity. Release the millstone from your neck by enacting a ceremony that gives your wishes solid form.

The old shamanistic traditions of Central Asia's nomadic tribes have never been completely forgotten. In rural Turkey, villagers still visit wishing trees to declare their unfulfilled hopes and dreams. They tie scraps of fabric around the branches and leave them there as *ziyaret* (pilgrimage) tokens, believing that their wishes will be taken up by the breeze and become true.

The wishing tree ceremony has its roots in ancient human history when pagan beliefs of nature-worship were common. In Turkey, mulberry trees are often chosen as wishing trees. Further east in Asia the banyan tree is the focus of this practice, while in Great Britain sycamores and hawthorns were regarded as lucky by the Celts and are visited by those seeking to fulfil their dreams.

You don't need to hold a certain spiritual belief to use a wishing tree. Sometimes it's enough just to articulate your hopes to restore balance in your life. Write down your wishes on a ribbon and tie it to a tree branch, offering it to the world as a votive token. By formally expressing your wishes you may find it simpler to see how they can be realised.

index

acknowledgements

PUBLISHING DIRECTOR Piers Pickard
PUBLISHER Ben Handicott
COMMISSIONING EDITOR Bridget Blair
EDITORS Nadine Davidoff, Amanda Williamson
DESIGN Mark Adams, Leon Mackie
LAYOUT DESIGNERS Nicholas Colicchia, Clara Monitto
THANKS Ryan Evans, Larissa Frost, Kylie McLaughlin

WRITTEN BY Johanna Ashby (p115, 119), James
Bainbridge (p89), Joe Bindloss (p21, 35, 57), Bridget Blair
(p15), Paul Bloomfield (p23, 103, 113), Piera Chen (p25),
Nigel Chin (p51), Mark Elliott (p65), Sarah Gilbert (p17,
67, 87, 99, 123), Will Gourlay (p45, 59), Tienlon Ho (p117),
Jessica Lee (p69, 125), Alex Leviton (introduction, p11, 47,
53, 71, 79, 107), Shawn Low (p95), Emily Matchar (p111,
73), Gabi Mocatta (p29, 39, 49, 81), Rose Mulready (p13,
19, 31, 55, 83), Simon Richmond (p37), Daniel Robinson
(p33), Tamara Sheward (p109, 121), Sarina Singh (p43),
Phillip Tang (p75, 77, 85, 91), Caroline Veldhuis (p93, 97,
105), Steve Waters (p61), Penny Watson (p27)

ILLUSTRATIONS Mat Edwards (p18, 54, 114), Luci
Everett (p38, 68), Marco Ferrara (p26, 30, 64), Cyril Hahn
(p16, 66, 80, 112, 122), Kathy Heaser (p44, 52, 110), David
Heffernan (p70, 92, 124), Andy Lewis (p12, 22, 28, 32, 48,
56), Darren Pryce (p24, 36, 42, 74, 78, 86, 88, 116, 118,
120), Sophia Touliatou (p96), Felipe Ubila (p60, 72), Bill
Wood (p14, 46, 76, 94), Andrew Yeoh (p104)

PHOTOGRAPHS Getty Images (p10, 34, 58, 90, 102, 107,
108), iStockphoto (p20, 50, 82, 84, 98)

PRINTED IN CHINA
10 9 8 7 6 5 4 3 2 1

CALM December 2013
PUBLISHED BY Lonely Planet Publications Pty Ltd
ABN 36 005 607 983
90 Maribyrnong St, Footscray, Victoria 3011, Australia
lonelyplanet.com
ISBN 978 1 74321 845 7
Text © Lonely Planet Publications Pty Ltd 2013
photos & illustrations © as indicated 2013

LONELY PLANET OFFICES
AUSTRALIA – Locked Bag 1, Footscray, Victoria 3011
Phone 03 8379 8000 Fax 03 8379 8111
Email talk2us@lonelyplanet.com.au
USA – 150 Linden St, Oakland, CA 94607
Phone 510 250 6400 Toll Free 800 275 8555 Fax 510 893 8572
Email info@lonelyplanet.com
UK – Media Centre, 201 Wood Lane, London W12 7TQ
Phone 020 8433 1333 Fax 020 8702 0112
Email go@lonelyplanet.co.uk